It's hard to be what you can't see
A project celebrating the achievements of women working in the law in Northern Ireland who have forged a path

By Susie Rea

GW00706106

Contents

Preface

The Artist

The Project

The Inspiration

Part I
It's hard to be what you can't see

Part II
Be what you see

Preface

A few years ago, the touring V&A exhibition 'Shoes: Pleasure and Pain' was heavily criticised for failing to call out the hobbling of women by shoes that inflict pain, permanent disfiguration and, ultimately, control. Many women of my generation, who were the first in our families to enter the legal sphere, had to learn not to be hobbled — by others or by ourselves — as we stumbled into an alien workplace. I was a slow learner. Almost 43 years ago, when I was one of two new lecturers appointed to the Law School at Queen's (the other was a man), I was surprised to learn that my duties included the making of the academic staff's morning coffee and the collection of the associated monies. This task, I was informed, always fell to the youngest female lecturer. It says something of the times, and my lack of spunk, that I did this for two years until the next woman appointed to the faculty said 'no' and called for fresh thinking. I did, however, draw the line at making the new curtains for the faculty meeting room when, without embarrassment, a male Dean asked me to do so.

Was it a case of 'you can't be what you can't see', to use Marian Wright Edelman's words? Not quite. When I came up to Queen's as an undergraduate, the Dean of the Faculty of Law was Professor Claire Palley, a distinguished and well-published public lawyer. If it had ever entered my head that Law School was no place for women – it didn't – her presence and personal authority would have banished such an idea. But what we were not told was that she was the first female law professor in the United Kingdom. Why did Queen's not take noticeable pride in the breaking of that glass ceiling? Denial of women's achievements is just another form of hobbling.

Congratulations are due to all those involved in the Women in Law initiative for their commitment to the values underpinning the Athena SWAN charter. In this landmark year which marks the centenary of the Sex Disqualification (Removal) Act 1919, it is important to stop, acknowledge and celebrate what women have achieved in professions where we are relative newcomers. As the National Women's History Alliance puts it: 'Our history is our strength.' This inspiring collection of letters from high-achieving women in the law to their younger selves does just that. But, as some of the contributors note, it is also important to remember the aspiring women of previous generations for whom all doors were closed. We owe it to them to continue to strive for gender equality in and under the law. Furthermore, as Susan Atkins and Brenda Hoggett argue in their recent re-issue of *Women and the Law* (first published in 1984), these gains can soon be lost and fresh challenges to gender equality can emerge. As they put it, 'A feminist focus remains as necessary today, for men as well as women, as it was thirty years ago.' A timely reminder for the younger contributors to this publication, young women setting out on their legal careers, who have written letters of encouragement to their older selves.

And what of the future? I look to Marian Wright Edelman, founder of the Children's Defense Fund (USA) and the inspiration for this publication, for the final word. To all of the contributors here, and to everyone fighting to remove inequality as one of the greatest barriers to justice, Wright Edelman's message is that there is no going back. We keep moving forward.

Norma Dawson, CBE
Professor Emeritus
Queen's University Belfast

The Artist

Susie Rea
Artist, Northern Irish, born 1977.

Susie Rea was brought up in Belfast. She read History at Cambridge University before studying Fine Art at Central Saint Martins College of Art and Design, London. After living for almost a decade in London, she relocated home to Belfast in 2007, where she now lives and works. She combines her fine art and commercial photographic practices with teaching and research at Ulster University, Belfast, where she is currently studying for a PhD with practice.

The School of Law commissioned this project in 2018 as part of its ongoing Athena SWAN work. The brief was to create original artwork(s) to visualise and celebrate women working in all aspects of the law in Northern Ireland, including the future generation of legal professionals, as represented by the School's student body. Working with Athena SWAN Champion, Dr Kathryn McNeilly, Susie Rea aims, through the project, to focus our attention on the importance of strong female role models, in their capacity as both pathfinders and leaders.

The Project

This project stems from the School of Law's commitment to the Athena SWAN Charter for gender equality, and its recognition of the importance of celebrating the successes of women in a visible way. It marks both the centenary of women's suffrage (1918), and one hundred years since the Sex Disqualification (Removal) Act (1919), an amendment to the law which sought to ensure against the disqualification of women by 'sex or marriage from the exercise of public function'. This commission therefore comes at a watershed moment and serves to celebrate the progress that has been made through the lives of a group of remarkable women – both professionals and students – who have forged a path.

The concept for the project was born out of a simple idea: to visualise these women in a way that is relatable to those who will follow in their footsteps. The students who will pass through the halls of the School of Law at Queen's University may find it hard to imagine themselves in positions of responsibility, influence or power, from which they could make a positive impact on the world. This project aims to show these young people that the judges, lawyers, teachers, politicians and policy makers of today were the students of yesterday, just like them.

Fittingly, the quotation that lends its name to Part I of this commission – 'It's hard to be what you can't see' – was coined by a female lawyer. Marian Wright Edelman, founder and President Emerita of the Children's Defense Fund in the United States, is a fascinating role model for current students. The first black woman admitted to the Mississippi bar, she has fought for the rights of vulnerable groups throughout her career. As a female and as a woman of colour she is a trailblazer. As we look to the future, her words are a gentle reminder of the need not just for gender equality within the institutions of the law in Northern Ireland, but also for greater diversity.

The Inspiration

Marian Wright Edelman
Founder and President Emerita of the Children's Defense Fund (CDF), Washington, D.C., USA

Marian Wright Edelman is a civil rights activist and founder of the Children's Defense Fund in Washington DC. The first black woman admitted to the Mississippi bar, Wright Edelman is a graduate of Spelman College and Yale Law School. She began her career as director of the Legal Defense and Educational Fund Office of the NAACP in Jackson, Mississippi, before moving to Washington, D.C. where she took up a role as counsel to the Poor People's Campaign, that Dr Martin Luther King Jr. began organising before his death. She founded the Washington Research Project in 1969, a public-interest law firm monitoring federal programmes for low-income families. Out of this initiative grew the CDF in 1973. Considered the most powerful children's lobby in the United States, the CDF secured the 1990 Act for Better Child Care, a seminal piece of federal legislation, which brought more than USD 3 billion into daycare facilites and other programmes. Wright Edelman is the recipient of many awards including the Presidential Medal of Freedom.

It's hard to be what you can't see

Part I

Claire Archbold, BL
Deputy Departmental Solicitor
to the Northern Ireland Executive

Claire Archbold is the Deputy Departmental Solicitor for
Northern Ireland, providing legal advice and services to the
Northern Ireland Departments and other public bodies.
She is the first woman to hold this post. She has undertaken
a range of policy and legal roles since joining Northern
Ireland Civil Service (NICS) in May 2000. She was Legal
Secretary to the Lord Chief Justice for six years and has also
spent time in policy roles in various different departments,
including the Department of Finance and Personnel, the
Office of the First Minister and Deputy First Minister, and
the Office of Law Reform. A qualified mediator, she has a
past history as an academic and as a practising barrister.
She is Vice-Chair of RelateNI and an external member of
the Department of Health's Audit and Risk Committee.
She sits occasionally as a District Judge in the County
Court and as a High Court Master. She is active within the
Law Society Women's Mentoring Scheme and the NICS
Mentoring Circles scheme.

Dear Claire,

It seems like no time since you arrived at Queen's, with a fresh bile pad, a keen sense of justice, no lawyers in the family, no real clue about what career you wanted. You hated the first term of law — everyone did — but there was a moment in Professor Hatfield's constitutional law lecture when you could see yourself enjoying this. And that was enough to

The m   e degree.
Over coffee   ramshackle
Claremont   s; what you
really tho   e well-spent —
those pass   elive when
you feel cl   , but they
are a route   thentically.

When   rthwhile, and
entirely unsu   itors or
barristers   se seemed
to think,   tute, and
then, we s

If you   ore about
your skills   be happiest
and most   ? Perhaps
that would

The jo   ven into the
Civil Service   most are
public law   o achieve.
The skills taught in the Law School are only part of what you will need. Character builds on the journey. More people remember integrity and kindness than clever arguments.

Don't get in your own way. Don't hold yourself back. It will take you a while. Maybe it takes everyone a while. But you will come to recognise the voice in your head that says, "Who do you think you are, trying to do this?" You will be 49 when you hear Lady Hale tell

Dear Claire,

It seems like no time since you arrived at Queen's, with a fresh file pad, a keen sense of justice, no lawyers in the family, no real clue about what career you wanted. You hated the first term of law – everyone did – but there was a moment in Professor Hadfield's constitutional law lecture when you could see yourself enjoying this. And, that was enough to keep you there.

The most important thing you did might not have been the degree. Over coffee in the Great Hall, in late night discussions in the ramshackle Claremont Street flat, you and your friends tested your opinions; what you really thought against what you had been told. That was time well-spent — those passions and values will be your guides — you will feel most alive when you feel closest to them. You will keep testing them, adjusting them, but they are a route map that will motivate you and allow you to live authentically.

When you graduated, you were bursting to do something worthwhile and entirely unsure what it might be. Those whose parents were solicitors or barristers seemed so assured in their choice of law. Everyone else seemed to think, well we've done a law degree, so now we go to the Institute, and then, we suppose, into practice. That's what people expect.

If you knew what I know now, would you have thought more about your skills and aptitudes, realising earlier that where you will be happiest and most effective is not at the bar, but in the public service? Perhaps that would miss the point. Every day is a school day.

The journey will take you from the bar to academia, then in to the Civil Service, where you will find that the things you enjoy most are public law, policy-making, leading a team, empowering others to achieve. The skills taught in the Law School are only part of what you will need.

Character builds on the journey. More people remember integrity and kindness than clever arguments.

Don't get in your own way. Don't hold yourself back. It will take you a while. Maybe it takes everyone a while. But you will come to recognise the voice in your head that says, 'Who do you think you are, trying to do this?' You will be forty-nine when you hear Lady Hale tell a roomful of women lawyers that she hears that voice too. Her crisp, confident tones ring out: 'Everyone does. If they tell you they don't, they're lying'. And that will resolve the doubt. Be at the table on your own terms.

Celebrate those who share the journey with you. The friends you sat with in lectures, argued with over coffee, went inter-railing with — they will be the friends who stand with you at weddings, funerals, hospital bedsides, swearings-in. One will become your spouse. Graduation felt like an ending, but the journey was only starting. Work hard, be kind to everyone, including yourself. Enjoy it.

With love and confidence,

Claire

The Hon. Mrs Justice Keegan
Appointed to the High Court in Northern Ireland (2015)

Mrs Justice Keegan is currently Judge in Residence at Queen's. She was called to the Bar of Northern Ireland in 1994 and was appointed Queen's Counsel in 2006. She specialised in family law but retained a practice in both criminal law and judicial review. During her career at the bar Mrs Justice Keegan served as Vice Chair of the Bar of Northern Ireland, Chair of the Young Bar, Chair of the Family Bar Association, Chair of the Bar Charity Committee and she was a long-standing member of the Bar Professional Conduct Committee. In 2015, Mrs Justice Keegan was one of the first women appointed to the High Court in Northern Ireland.

I graduated in 1993 after studying law for four years at Queens. I actually wanted to be a teacher but I was encouraged to try law on the basis that it was a good degree to have. I did not come from a legal background but my parents supported me and allowed me the freedom to find my own way.

There w...
in my year...
trades. I n...
gradually a...
how I dire...
President of...
final year w...
and boss w...
my progress...
by la la...
support.

I am o...
particularly...
to look up...
to attend...
UCD in the...
up the ranks...
was to find a...
of pupil whe...
or trades...
her time.

During my time at Queens the legal profession in NI was dominated by men. That was a challenge for the large numbers of women qualifying however

Dear Siobhan,

After studying law for four years at Queen's you graduated in 1993. You actually wanted to be a teacher but were encouraged to try law on the basis that it was a good degree to have. You did not come from a legal background, but your parents supported you and allowed you the freedom to find your own way.

There were four other girls from your year at school at Queen's and along with the other good friends you made, you embraced student life; gradually adapting to the study of law, realising how diverse and dynamic it is. You were President of the Students' Law Society in your final year which meant you got to organise events and boss your friends around (so they say). Anyway, your progress through Queen's was sustained by a large measure of parental and peer support. Thinking of role models, particularly female role models, you had your aunt (now deceased) to look up to. She was the first in your family to attend university when she studied maths at University College Dublin in the 1950s. She became a teacher, rising up the ranks to be a school principal. Her ethos was to find and develop a skill for every level of pupil whether through academic work, sport or trades. She was ahead of her time.

During your time at Queen's the upper echelons of the legal profession in Northern Ireland were dominated by men. That was a challenge for the large numbers of women qualifying. However, over these years a conversation about the need for diversity within the profession was also happening. We owe a debt to these advocates for change (particularly women lawyers), many of whom did not fulfil their own ambitions, because they laid the groundwork for people like us who wanted to progress. I am glad that things have moved on and that there is a continued emphasis on removing impediments for women wanting to progress in professional life. I hope we offer some inspiration to young men and women that you can succeed in the legal profession. If we did it, they can.

If I have any other words of advice to offer you, they are these:

- Don't waste time worrying about things you cannot control.

- Do spend time thinking about how you can change things as a lawyer.

- Know your mind and don't be afraid to express your own view.

- Pick yourself up from the disappointments. Learn and try again.

- Work hard at law but not to the exclusion of your other interests and having some fun.

- You can achieve a lot if you believe in yourself.

Good luck,

Siobhan Keegan.

Judith Eve, CBE
Former Dean of the Faculty of Law at
Queen's University (1986—9)

Judith Eve is a qualified barrister and former Senior
Lecturer and Dean of the Faculty of Law. She is currently
part-time Legal Chair of The Appeals Service (NI). She
has served on the boards of many public bodies, mainly in
the areas of housing, health and recruitment regulation
— both to the Northern Ireland Civil Service and in the
public sector. Most recently, she was Chair of the board
of the Public Appointments Service (Ireland).

- respect the views of other people
- be caring and respectful in your treatment of others

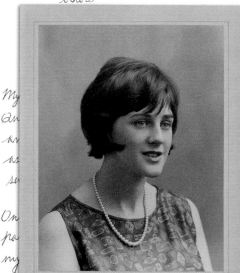

act on it

best, whatever

My ~~~~~ read law at
On ~~~~~ (ulty of law)
an ~~~~~ they have
as ~~~~~ ments,
se ~~~~~

On ~~~~~ veloped one
pa ~~~~~ e doubted
my ~~~~~ tainity or
ch ~~~~~ but in
homelife too.   If my immediate thought was
"I couldn't do that," yet I admitted to myself
that I was interested in trying to do so; I
would ask myself "Who is proposing that I should
put myself forward for this responsibility? Do
I trust their experience and judgment"

Dear Judith,

This has proved a challenging task. Given the opportunity, what would I say to my younger self preparing to leave school and move on to read law at Queen's University?

I considered writing information and advice about employment and career development, about friendships and relationships, about family life.

This trip led me down memory lane and encouraged me to reflect on what I have achieved since I left university. The various jobs and appointments I have held; the colleagues who have become friends; the expansion of my family with marriages and births; the relatives and friends who have passed away. What advice, received as a young person, would have helped me cope better with life?

These are some obvious guiding points:

- Be flexible and do not rigidly follow your plans as other people will impact on them and you.

- Take the opportunity to learn from mistakes and see them as a means for positive development.

- Respect the views of other people.

- Be caring and respectful in your treatment of others.

- Listen to your conscience and act on it.

- Always try to give of your best, whatever the tasks.

My parents raised my brother (who also read law at Queen's and also lectured in the Faculty of Law) and me with these values and they have assisted me to cope with new developments, successes, disappointments, stressors.

On reflection, I realised that I have developed one particular way of coping when I have doubted my ability to undertake a new opportunity or challenge, particularly in the workplace, but in home life too. If my immediate thought was, 'I couldn't do that' yet I admitted to myself that I was interested in trying to do so, I would ask myself, 'Who is proposing that I should put myself forward for this responsibility? Do I trust their experience and judgement? 'If the answer was yes, I would then tell myself 'You probably can do it well' and then I would go for it. Fortunately, that has worked for me.

So, in summary, the main piece of advice that I would give to my younger self is to trust the views and advice of people who know you — whether in the workplace or elsewhere — and whose judgment you respect.

Judith Eve

Monye Anyadike-Danes, QC
Co-Chair of the British Irish Commercial Bar Association &
member of the Northern Ireland Bar Pro Bono Committee

Monye Anyadike-Danes, has worked as a corporate and
commercial lawyer, and as a practising advocate for over
thirty years. She is a graduate of both the University of
Bristol and the University of Cambridge. She began her
career at 2 Temple Gardens, London, in 1981, where she
remains a member of chambers. She has practised in
Northern Ireland since 1997 and took silk in 2007. She is
also a member of the Bars of England & Wales, St Vincent
& the Grenadines, and the Republic of Ireland. She has
extensive experience in construction law, commercial law
and public procurement law. She also has a very well-
developed human rights and judicial review practice,
acting for individuals, organisations and public bodies.
She is the current UK chair of the British Irish Commercial
Bar Association and is an active member of the Bar
Council's Pro Bono committee. In addition she has been
a member of Justice since 2012, and Lawyers without
Borders since 2014.

Perhaps you are right to want to learn in your own way and develop your career through your own experiences.

Nevertheless,

'Whilst y   n behalf of
your clien   uth and
justice wh   houghts and
in your on   ich it is
now full   e to guide
you. Howe   y it now.
Learning t   long bar
rewarding

'For a clie   , and to
rely on yo   the law, in
all its com   ght you
here and   ng to
learn how   Ultimately,
though, a   t comes to
you and

There will be some circumstances in which the weight of the responsibility of living up to all of this feels very heavy. Do not worry. You will get through it and with more fun than you could ever imagine.

Mongeazo.

Dear Monye,

Perhaps you are right to want to learn in your own way and develop your career through your own experiences.

Nevertheless, these are my thoughts for you.

'Whilst you owe a duty to do all that you honourably can on behalf of your client, you also owe a duty to one higher cause of truth and justice which is paramount.' This is not an original thought and in your own time you will discover the judgment in which it is now fully expressed and it will become a touchstone to guide you. However, I should like you to have the benefit of it now. Learning to respond to these twin duties will be a life long but rewarding challenge.

'For a client to put their case completely in your hands, and to rely on you, is a true privilege.' A fascination with the law in all its complexities and inadequacies is what has brought you here, and you rightly anticipate that it will be exciting to learn how to apply it and be part of its development. Ultimately, though, all of that is only possible because a client comes to you and trusts you.

There will be some circumstances in which the weight of the responsibility of living up to all of this feels very heavy. Do not worry.

You will get through it and with more fun than you could ever imagine.

Mongeazo.

The Hon. Madam Justice McBride, DBE
Appointed to the High Court in Northern Ireland (2015)

Madam Justice McBride was called to the Bar of Northern
Ireland in 1989 and was appointed Queen's Counsel
in 2011. She specialised in chancery, family, civil and
international law. In 2006, she was appointed an Honorary
Lecturer at Queen's University in recognition of her long
service as a tutor and guest lecturer. She served as Vice
Chair of the Bar Council of Northern Ireland from 2012–14.
In 2015, Justice McBride was the first woman appointed to
the High Court of Northern Ireland.

Yes, you will meet many challenges along the
way. At times you will be tempted to give up and
walk away. You will not do this because you will
have the privilege of meeting some amazing
women, and

you but als

when the goo

of a wise sen

"If you want

you need to

away and w

history."

to my odv

· Be strong an

· Don't be afra
up when yo

· Work hard

· Always act with integrity

· Always be kind - it improves both the giver
and the receiver

· Be thankful for every good gift you have
received.

Dear Denise,

In this photo you are just about to leave school and go to Queen's University Belfast, to study law. Even though your mum has told you that you can be whatever you want to be you are not entirely convinced because you are just an ordinary girl from a small school in rural County Down and right now there are only a handful of female QCs and no female judges in Northern Ireland.

What you don't know now but will later discover is that you will see and be part of major changes in the legal profession. So, as you embark upon what is going to be an incredible journey, I want to give you some encouragement and advice.

Yes, you will meet many challenges along the way. At times you will be tempted to give up and walk away. You will not do this because you will have the privilege of meeting some amazing women, and men, who will not only inspire you but also support and encourage you when the going is tough. Never forget the advice given to you by a wise senior female barrister, 'If you want to change the legal profession you need to hang in there. Stay, don't walk away and who knows you might even make history'.

So, my advice to you is:

- Be strong and resilient.
- Don't be afraid to use your voice and speak up when you should.
- Work hard.
- Always act with integrity.
- Always be kind – it improves both the giver and the receiver.
- Be thankful for every good gift you have.

Use all your talents to make the world a better place, especially for those who are disadvantaged. Be humble –

like me you have lots to learn. But remember life is not just about work. Make sure you make time for friends and family and yourself. Take time to enjoy the simple pleasures in life like watching the waves crashing over the harbour wall on a stormy day, eating ice cream covered in hot chocolate sauce and laughing out loud.

So there you have it. Enjoy the journey and I hope that you too will be an inspiration to others.

With best wishes,

from an olde Densie.

Professor Monica McWilliams
Negotiator at the Belfast/Good Friday Agreement
and former Chief Commissioner of the Northern Ireland
Human Rights Commission

Monica McWilliams is Emeritus Professor in the Transitional
Justice Institute at the University of Ulster. She co-founded
the Northern Ireland Women's Coalition political party
and was one of the few women elected to the Multi-
Party Peace Negotiations, which led to the Good Friday/
Belfast Agreement in 1998. She served as a member of the
Northern Ireland Legislative Assembly from 1998 to 2003,
and was the Chief Commissioner of the Northern Ireland
Human Rights Commission from 2005 to 2011. She is one
of four members, and the only woman, on the Independent
Reporting Commission for the disbandment of paramilitary
organisations, appointed from 2017 to 2021.

The mid 1970's was the best of times and the worst
of times   was
not at pea   he
turmoil,   vive.
During the   ike,
when we   and
were placed   ged
to keep g   tered
the peace   iday
Agreement,   n
good stea

For a young woman from a farming background,
going to Queens opened up doors for me. Every
Summer, when term ended, we jumped on a plane
and headed to the New Jersey shore to earn
the much needed funds to support our adventures.
Driving a Pinto Runabout on Route 66 from
Philadelphia to San Francisco added another notch

Dear Monica,

The mid 1970s was the best of times and the worst of times to be a student. Northern Ireland was not at peace with itself but amidst all the turmoil, I learned to thrive as well as survive. During the 1974 Ulster Workers' Council Strike, when we had no food, electricity or transport and were placed under curfew, we somehow managed to keep going. Two decades later, when I entered the peace negotiations leading to the Good Friday Agreement, that resilience was to stand me in good stead.

For a young woman from a farming background, going to Queen's opened up doors for me. Every summer, when term ended, we jumped on a plane and headed to the New Jersey shore to earn the much needed funds to support our adventures. Driving a Pinto runabout on Route 66 from Philadelphia to San Francisco added another notch to my independence. When I won a scholarship to the University of Michigan, my educational tool box was fast filling up.

So, work hard and play hard. To keep that sense of balance through life is easier said than done. How I wish I could still fly up the left wing on the Dub playing field or captain the women's athletics team one more time.

I learned to fly my wings at Queen's and once I got going, I never stopped.

Monica Mc Williams

Noelle McGrenera, QC
Former Chair of the Bar Council of Northern Ireland and
former Treasurer of the Inn of Court of Northern Ireland

Noelle McGrenera was educated at Queen's University
Belfast. She was called to the bar in 1978 and took silk in
1999. She now works mainly in employment law, family
law and general civil law. Ms McGrenera is a former
Chairperson of the Family Bar Association of Northern
Ireland. From 2006—8 she served as Chairperson of the
Executive Council of the Inn of Court and Bar Council
of Northern Ireland, and was the first woman to be
elected to that post. She was appointed a Bencher in
2004 and served as Treasurer of the Inn in 2014; the
first woman to so do since the foundation of the Inn.
In 2015, she was made an Honorary Bencher of the
Honorable Society of Middle Temple. She is a fellow of the
International Academy of Trial Lawyers and a Fellow of the
International Association of Barristers. She currently is the
representative of the Bar Council of Northern Ireland on
the Judicial Appointments Commission.

Family life — now there is a conundrum. You will marry the boy in the duffle coat who came up from Dublin to go to the Institute and he will be at your side as you go on to have four wonderful children of whom you are both very proud.

The feeling  never have yo... can and it ... Further advice g... time off to a... never took.

You will be... bring you great...

Support will... open to taking...

Above all ... a student. They ... be there on th... wrong in ...

And finally, never, ever buy a purple corduroy suit and wear it into court!

Noelle McGuinness.

Dear Noelle,

You graduated from QUB and started at the Institute of Professional Legal Studies in September 1977, opting to choose the bar course.

Your family had no connections in law and you were fortunate to get a really good Master at the bar, Tim Ferriss, through sources that had nothing to do with law.

So looking back, I admire the mixture of naivety and courage that led you to choose a career as a barrister in Northern Ireland when women were still very thin on the ground.

You arrived at the bar in September 1978 and your year had the largest number of women in the call up to that point in time. So began a career that has lasted, to date, over forty years!

Tim Ferriss advised you from the get-go to always accept a brief even if it appeared outside your comfort zone. That was good, if very challenging advice, notwithstanding the occasional stomach-churning moments in court when an inquiring judge appeared to question your expertise in a particular sphere of the law. So those early days of trips to far flung petty sessions for dubious contests or travelling to remote county courts for a civil bill about rights of way over a particular lane way had to be endured and accepted.

However, try not to allow yourself to be talked into giving a client a lift all the way back to Belfast thereby allowing a tedious post mortem of the day's activities! Do not be put off by the number of times the client tells you you look too young to be a barrister. Just carry on. It will pass, believe me, and all too soon.

Do not either become too upset when a solicitor tells you, despite having won a case, that you will not be getting the brief on the appeal because he has been admonished by his firm for briefing a Catholic, and a woman at that, in the first place. Such days will also happily pass.

Always do your very best for the client and prepare well. You are not the sort of person to wing it. Try to empathise with the client whilst remembering that at times a full and frank analysis of the weaknesses of their case is an absolute must to discharge your professional duty to them.

The Bar was and still is an open and welcoming place so join in its activities, clubs and representations.

A wise judge once told your opposing counsel, 'Mr. X, you will have many clients in your career but only one reputation.' Wise words indeed. Sadly, that particular counsel has long since left the Bar.

Family life – now there is a conundrum. You will marry the boy in the duffle coat who came up from Dublin to go to the Institute and he will be at your side as you go on to have four wonderful children of whom you are both very proud.

The feeling of guilt as a working mother will never leave you. Just balance matters as best you can and it will all work out in the end. Further advice I do not feel qualified to give. Taking time off for a long maternity period was a rest I never took. You will become a granny in 2018 which will bring you great joy.

Support will come from unexpected places and be open to taking help and advice.

Above all else, retain the friendships you made as a student. They will sustain you, make you laugh and be there on the days when it has all gone terribly wrong in court despite your best endeavours!

And finally, never, ever buy a purple corduroy suit and wear it into court!

Noelle Mc Guinness.

The Hon. Ms Justice Doherty, CBE
Former Judge of the High Court and Court of Appeal
of Sierra Leone

Ms Justice Doherty is a member of the Bars of Northern
Ireland, New South Wales and Papua New Guinea (PNG).
In 1987 she was appointed a Principal Magistrate for the
Momase Region and then as a Judge of the Supreme and
National Courts of PNG. For eleven years she was the
first and only woman judge in the South Pacific Islands
region. From 2003, at the request of the Commonwealth,
she served as a Judge of the High Court and the Court of
Appeals of Sierra Leone following the civil war. In 2005, she
was appointed judge of the Special Court for Sierra Leone
by the United Nations. In Northern Ireland, she has served
as Parole Commissioner and as part-time Chair of Appeal
Services since 2002. She has spoken widely on human
rights and women's rights in various countries and holds
several honorary positions.

Learn to challenge, calmly and simply. Many times you will hear minor officials using an excuse for inaction or trying to force their will on others by saying "its the law!". Ask [...] [...]nd up to male colle[...] stereotypical att[...] against women. [...] bull them into [...]

Try to stop regre[...] to do. It cannot [...]ing "The man/wom[...] [...] made anything. [...]d that your rel[...] support, often a[...] dangerous places. [...]h out to them, w[...]ds will alert you [...] do something. [...] need it.

Be careful too. [...]er and the first woman judge. Believe it or not that will be you.

I know you have hopes for the future but life is going to dish out something different. It will not always be easy to accept. Surprisingly it will make a difference for others.

Teresa

Dear Teresa,

Well, you finally got that degree you aspired to for years despite being told 'you're not fit to clip threads' and coming from a humble background. You'll be surprised where it will bring you, but do not forget where you came from. It will remind you that not everyone gets the same chance of an education. You will meet many such intelligent resourceful people. You must learn to stand up for yourself; you will be doing a lot of standing up for others, especially women. You should learn to say 'no' but you never do and that will cause you to travel for miles on dirt roads to remote persons and courts, and lead to confrontation with officials in many countries from Papua New Guinea and Guyana to Sierra Leone.

You will find that bad administration, abuse of position (especially minor positions), and male domination of women lead to abuse of human rights. If that is not dealt with, it increases, then becomes taken for granted by abuser and abused.

You can use the law to change this. It will take some ingenuity. Learn not to rush in. Research, prepare and prepare again. You will find that there is an answer; maybe in a constitution. If a customary rule is applied only to women who are punished for breaching it while men can do the same without censure then this offends equality provisions and is unconstitutional. Look into the international conventions and treaties. Not just those you learnt at university, there are plenty more. Their provisions can be used when interpreting domestic law. You will be applying a lot of them, particularly when you come to deal with complex cases including war crimes and crimes against humanity.

Learn to challenge, calmly and simply. Many times you will hear minor officials using an excuse for inaction or trying to force their will on others by saying, 'It's the law.' Ask which law, that will silence them. Stand up to male colleagues who persist in upholding stereotypical attitudes to sexual and other offences against women. Don't be confrontational, it will lull them into a false sense of security.

Try to stop regretting things you got wrong or failed to do. It cannot be changed. Remember the Irish saying 'the man/woman who never made a mistake never made anything.' Accept help from others. You will find that your newly acquired husband will be a support, often driving and watching for you in dangerous places. Other women will support you — reach out to them. Women's organisations and individuals will alert you to problems and will rely on you to do something. They will care for you when you need it.

Be careful too. Many men will resent a woman lawyer and the first woman judge. Believe it or not that will be you.

I know you have hopes for the future but life is going to chuck out something different. It will not always be easy to accept. Surprisingly it will make a difference for others.

Teresa

be
what
you
see

Part II

Dear Abena,

The knowledge you are acquiring outside the classroom walls is a good start, continue... As I always say, your only limitation in life is when you refuse to speak. To speak is power and power is what gives you the authority to begin the change you seek.

As a committee member of QUB Gender Network and Women In Law, keep the momentum to learn from these platforms. As you climb the ladder of empowerment, promise to be your source of strength as God has made you - be strong & persevere. The projects you have started will gain the world's attention.

You have received encouragement from beautiful people around you. Abena... just as you are... You are enough! Keep this spirit active. Remember your humble beginnings and always empower those behind you.

With Love,
Abena

Abena Adusepoku
Queen's University Belfast, 2016—19

Dear Alex,

The woman sitting in that photo is on the cusp of experiencing all the love, joy and challenges of motherhood. It is better and more awesome than you could imagine. Do not underestimate the challenge of balancing childcare and finishing your dissertation. These experiences confirm the importance of the feminist struggle for equality and solidarity for women in higher education.

The woman in the photo is proud of the work that she has contributed as co-founder (with Maria Pimentel) to Women in Law QUB. Never lose that ambition and desire to make the world a little bit BETTER. You have done this by creating a group that supports women to be ambitious in their legal education and future careers.

Embrace the uncertainty you are feeling as you embark on your life after law school. If it feels scary, it is probably worth doing. No one grows in the comfort zone!

All my love,
Alex

Alexandra Born
Queen's University Belfast, 2015—19

Dear Doreen,

Here I am in this big, empty room reminiscing. Today is 1st of March, 2019 and you have clung to the lead against all the odds. I am proud of you and everything you have achieved. With determination and hardwork, you won the 2018 Client counselling competition for Queens University and represented Northern Ireland at the International level with your friend, Abena. Now you are the National Representative for Ghana at ICCC and a postgraduate representative for QUB women in the Law Lean-in circle. Crazy right!! You thought you wouldn't survive yet here you are in your final year Law school, pushing through your weakness with strength.

If you are reading this letter, this is it, we stuck it out this far together. I hope you are fighting for Justice, marching to freedom songs, and a champion of change. I hope you know the choices that you made will become the very choices that make you who you are. So, please be informed, ask a lot of questions before any decision.

The word 'accomplishment' means reaching your dreams for us, Remember! I hope you know your best efforts may not solve the world's problems but are enough to make many things right in this world. So be easy on yourself but don't ever give up on any of our dreams. Girl, we are not quitters!!! Be proud of the woman you have become and yet to be. God be with you and stay focused.

Forever us,

Doreen

Doreen Awuah
Queen's University Belfast, 2016–19

Dear Madeleine,

I know the past year was one of the most difficult and challenging so far, but you're still here and you're doing amazing. I'm so proud of you. You've learnt a lot, you've lost some friends, you've made new ones. You have an absolutely brilliant team of women supporting you wherever you go. Appreciate them.

Recognise that your family is who you can count on. They're always there for you, when you're at your lowest to get you back on your feet and when you're at your best, to celebrate you. Celebrate your successes, no matter how small. Be proud of what you have achieved so far. Don't be so modest all the time. Last year you dreamt of mooting externally, this year you're doing it.

Don't overthink every situation, it won't help you in that moment. Keep writing and keep dreaming. Take care of yourself, you need it too. Know your worth, the right people will meet you there. And lastly, remind yourself why you're doing this. I believe in you.

Madeleine, love the life you're living. I hope, wherever you are, you're genuinely happy. I loved the old you and I love the present you. But I love the woman you're becoming even more.

Love,

Madeleine

Madeleine Huber
Queen's University Belfast, 2017—20

Dear Maria,

I am so proud of you and how far you have come to achieve all your goals! You never let your circumstances define you. Now that you have graduated top of your JD class of 2019, anything is possible. Take everything you have learned from studying law, creating QUB Women in Law and competing as a negotiator for the ADR society — start anew! wherever you go, you will always have what it takes to succeed! You are enough! You are a powerhouse! Be kind to yourself and have faith. Follow your intuition!

With Love,

Maria

Maria Pimentel
Queen's University Belfast, 2015—18

To the barrister in my life

First published in 2019 by
Queen's University
University Road
Belfast BT7 1NN

Designed by Lisa Dynan

Printed in Northern Ireland by W & G Baird

A CIP catalogue for this book is available from the British Library.

ISBN 978 1 90913 189 7

www.susierea.com

Special thanks to the Law School at Queen's University for
commissioning the artworks and to Dr Kathryn McNeilly, Project
Liaison, and Leah Treanor, Project Assistant, who facilitated the
creative process with vision. Thanks also to each of the participants
for their trust in and openness to the concept underpinning the work.
Without their help the project would not have been possible. Finally,
appreciation should be extended to Lisa Dynan for going beyond
the call, to Helen Wright for her professional eye, and to Michelle
McKeown for pointing out the obvious.